M257 Unit 9
UNDERGRADUATE COMPUTING

Putting Java to work

Internet programming

Unit 9

This publication forms part of an Open University course M257 *Putting Java to work*. Details of this and other Open University courses can be obtained from the Student Registration and Enquiry Service, The Open University, PO Box 197, Milton Keynes MK7 6BJ, United Kingdom: tel. +44 (0)870 333 4340, email general-enquiries@open.ac.uk

Alternatively, you may visit the Open University website at http://www.open.ac.uk where you can learn more about the wide range of courses and packs offered at all levels by The Open University.

To purchase a selection of Open University course materials visit http://www.ouw.co.uk, or contact Open University Worldwide, Michael Young Building, Walton Hall, Milton Keynes MK7 6AA, United Kingdom for a brochure. tel. +44 (0)1908 858785; fax +44 (0)1908 858787; email ouwenq@open.ac.uk

The Open University
Walton Hall, Milton Keynes
MK7 6AA

First published 2007. Second edition 2008.

Edited, designed and typeset by The Open University.

Printed and bound in the United Kingdom by Hobbs the Printers Ltd.

ISBN 978 0 7492 1994 9

2.1

The paper used in this publication contains pulp sourced from forests independently certified to the Forest Stewardship Council® (FSC®) principles and criteria. Chain of custody certification allows the pulp from these forests to be tracked to the end use (see www.fsc-uk.org).

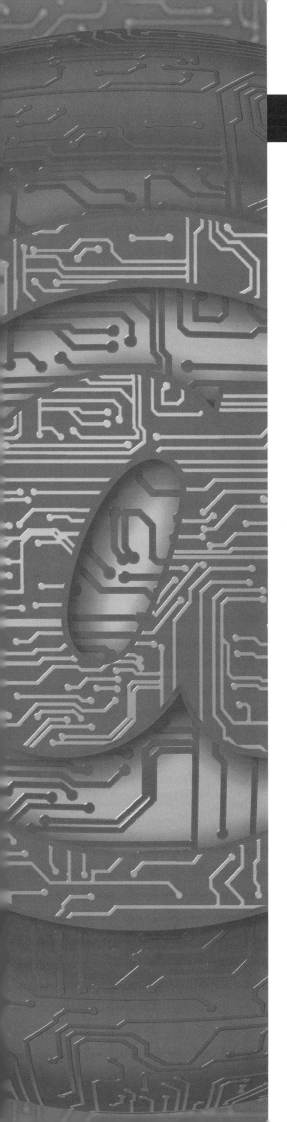

CONTENTS

1	Introduction	5
2	Accessing the web using Java	6
	2.1 The URL class	6
3	Distributed systems	9
	3.1 Advantages and disadvantages of distributed systems	9
	3.2 Distributed system architectures	9
	3.3 Client–server computing on the internet	12
4	Internet and web protocols	13
	4.1 Web servers	13
	4.2 Internet protocols	13
	4.3 Application protocols	15
	4.4 Connections over the internet	17
5	Addressing on the internet	19
	5.1 Symbolic addressing	19
	5.2 IP addressing	19
	5.3 The Internet Domain Name Service	20
	5.4 Ports and sockets	20
	5.5 Addressing resources on the web	21
6	Programming with sockets	24
	6.1 Sockets on the client	24
	6.2 Sockets on the server	24
7	A simple client–server example	28
	7.1 Simple server	28
	7.2 Simple client	30
8	A name service	33
	8.1 The server code	33
	8.2 The client code	38
9	Serving multiple clients	43
10	Datagram communication	47
	10.1 The client code	47
	10.2 The server code	49
11	Summary	53
	Index	55

M257 COURSE TEAM

M257 *Putting Java to work* was adapted from M254 *Java everywhere*.

M254 was produced by the following team.

Martin Smith, Course Team Chair and Author

Anton Dil, Author

Brendan Quinn, Author

Janet Van der Linden, Academic Editor

Barbara Poniatowska, Course Manager

Ralph Greenwell, Course Manager

Alkis Stavrinides, External Assessor, Coventry University

Critical readers

Pauline Curtis, Associate Lecturer

David Knowles, Associate Lecturer

Robin Walker, Associate Lecturer

Richard Walker, Associate Lecturer

The M257 adaptation was produced by:

Darrel Ince, Course Team Chair and Author

Richard Walker, Consultant Author and Critical Reader

Matthew Nelson, Critical Reader

Barbara Poniatowska, Course Manager

Ralph Greenwell, Course Manager

Alkis Stavrinides, External Assessor, Coventry University

Media development staff

Andrew Seddon, Media Project Manager

Garry Hammond, Editor

Ian Blackham, Editor

Anna Edgley-Smith, Editor

Jenny Brown, Freelance Editor

Andrew Whitehead, Designer and Graphic Artist

Glen Derby, Designer

Phillip Howe, Compositor

Lisa Hale, Compositor

Thanks are due to the Desktop Publishing Unit of the Faculty of Mathematics and Computing.

1 Introduction

So far, we have described many features of the Java programming language that are broadly equivalent to those in other programming languages. This unit marks a change in that we will consider some of the more distinctive aspects of Java, which make it very popular for internet-related programming.

We will describe how to use Java to program internet-based applications, such as those associated with ecommerce or internet chat rooms.

In this unit, we aim to:

▶ show how programs can access data from websites;

▶ outline how the internet is structured and how it works;

▶ explain the roles of clients and servers, and how to program them;

▶ demonstrate how servers can handle multiple clients;

▶ look at connectionless communication using datagrams.

First, we look at an example program to see how easy it is to access data from the web using Java.

2 Accessing the web using Java

In this section, we demonstrate with a simple example how we can use Java to access websites. In later sections, we shall look at some of the underlying technology involved in using the internet for such things. Although the technical details of this are rather complex, Java makes it easy to write programs to access data on the web by providing powerful classes in its standard packages. In particular, the important Java class URL provides facilities for accessing resources that are identified by their uniform resource locator or URL.

Many people are broadly familiar with the idea of a URL, such as:

```
http://www.open.ac.uk
```

You may be used to thinking of a URL as a web page address, in this case the address of the home page of The Open University. However, the concept of a URL is more general than this and includes other kinds of resources. We shall return to consider URLs in more detail later in this unit.

2.1 The URL class

The class URL has a number of constructors that allow the programmer to create uniform resource locators. For the moment, we consider only the simplest constructor – a single argument constructor that creates a URL object from its string description. For example:

```
URL openUniversity = new URL("http://www.open.ac.uk");
```

An important method, called openStream, opens a stream to a web resource such as a web page and allows the programmer to access the contents of the resource.

The following code is for a class called WebReader that accesses a website and displays the contents of the home page of the site. If you execute the associated test program, you will see the HTML for the home page of The Open University displayed on System.out.

```java
import java.net.*;
import java.io.*;

public class WebReader
{
    private BufferedReader fromWebSite;
    private String webAddress;

    public WebReader (String address)
    {
        webAddress = address;
        try
        {
            System.out.println("Trying to contact " + webAddress);
            URL selectedURL = new URL(webAddress);
            fromWebSite = new BufferedReader(
                            new InputStreamReader(
                                selectedURL.openStream())));
        }
        catch (MalformedURLException me)
        {
            System.out.println("Malformed URL found " + me);
        }
        catch (IOException io)
        {
            System.out.println("Problems connecting " + io);
        }
    }

    /* Read and display source contents of web page.
     Uses BufferedReader fromWebSite, set up by constructor. */
    public void print ()
    {
        String lineRead;
        System.out.println(" --- URL: " + webAddress);
        try
        {
            // read from website, one line at a time
            lineRead = fromWebSite.readLine();
            while (lineRead ! = null)
            {
                System.out.println(lineRead);
                lineRead = fromWebSite.readLine();
            }
            fromWebSite.close();
        }
        catch (IOException io)
        {
            System.out.println("Problems reading " + io );
        }
        System.out.println(" --- End of URL: " + webAddress);
    }
}
```

The class `WebReader` has a constructor and a public method `print`. The constructor instantiates a `URL` object for the address supplied as a `String` argument. It then accesses the input stream for this `URL` object and uses this to create a `BufferedReader` for inputting character data from the resource.

Two possible exceptions could be generated in the constructor. A `MalformedURLException` could occur when the `URL` object is constructed and an `IOException` could arise when the stream is associated with the web resource. These are handled by separate `catch` clauses – it is important that the `MalformedURLException` clause occurs first.

The `print` method reads from the resource (in this case, a web page) one line at a time and displays each line on `System.out`. The method terminates when there are no more lines to read, indicated by the `readLine` method of the buffered reader returning a null reference. Before the method terminates, it closes the stream `fromWebSite`.

The following class shows how we use a `WebReader` object:

```
public class TestWebReader
{
    public static void main (String[] args)
    {
        WebReader wr = new WebReader("http://www.open.ac.uk");
        wr.print();
    }
}
```

The `main` method creates a `WebReader` object for the Open University home page and invokes the `print` method to display the source (that is, the HTML) for this page. You can compare this output with the result you obtain when you visit this site using a browser – select a browser menu option to display the web page source.

Activity 9.1
Testing the `WebReader` class.

SAQ 1

(a) Why do the `catch` clauses in the constructor of the `WebReader` class need to be in that specific order?

(b) What would happen if they were swapped around?

ANSWERS ....

(a) The `MalformedURLException` class is a subclass of the `IOException` class. Recall from our discussion of exceptions in a previous unit that a `catch` clause for a particular type of exception will catch all exceptions of that class and of any of its subclasses. So the `MalformedURLException` clause must come first if we want to separately identify (and handle) this type of exception.

(b) If the `catch` clause for the `IOException` came first, it would catch any `MalformedURLException` objects as well as more general `IOException` objects. The second `catch` clause (for `MalformedURLException`) would never be used, and the compiler would flag an error due to unreachable code.

---

3 Distributed systems

A **distributed system** is a collection of computers at different locations, connected by communications links. The functions and data of the system are distributed across these computers, which are known as **hosts**. The internet is an enormous distributed system – most distributed systems are much smaller and typically serve the needs of one company or department within an organization.

3.1 Advantages and disadvantages of distributed systems

There are a number of reasons why computer systems are distributed and they are as follows.

▶ *Efficiency.* By placing data close to a user, access to that data can be fast. For example, an ecommerce system that keeps stock details of all the products sold by a collection of department stores could keep data relating to each individual store on the local computer found at a store, rather than in some central computer.

▶ *Ease of upgrading.* When demands on a system grow, more processing power and storage are usually required. A distributed system can cope with this relatively easily by having more and more computers added to it.

▶ *Reliability.* A distributed system can be developed in which some of the hosts in the system can act as a backup to other hosts in case they malfunction, thus helping to maintain a continuous service.

▶ *Ability to support a number of platforms.* A distributed system that communicates via a set of standard protocols such as those found in the internet can be built up from a number of computers running a variety of platforms, for example Linux, Windows and Macintosh operating systems.

Protocols are discussed in Section 4.

Hence there are a number of persuasive reasons for organizing a system in a distributed fashion. There are however drawbacks, which are as follows.

▶ *Performance.* If not designed properly, distributed systems can suffer from poor performance: the connections between hosts in a distributed system are a number of orders of magnitude slower than the internal wiring speeds of a computer.

▶ *Security.* The internet is an open system. Consequently, security can be a major problem: not only are the details of the various protocols used in the internet public, but also the messages sent over the internet usually traverse publicly accessible communication lines. It is also easier for viruses and other undesirable software to spread across a distributed system.

3.2 Distributed system architectures

There are a number of different **system architectures**, or ways of structuring the network of computers in a distributed system. For example, each computer in the system may be defined as either a **client** or a **server**. A server is normally a powerful computer that manages data, printers or network traffic. A client is normally a PC or workstation on which users run application programs or user interface code. Clients request services from servers, as shown in Figure 1, where a web client sends requests to a web server using a special language defined by the **HyperText Transfer Protocol** (**HTTP**). We shall explain HTTP in Section 4.

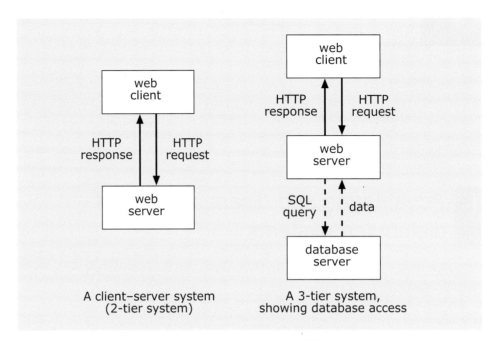

Figure 1   Examples of 2-tier and 3-tier system architectures

Client–server architectures are sometimes called 2-tier architectures. Architectures may have three or more tiers, leading to the so-called *n*-tier architecture, where *n* is 2, 3, 4 or more. Each of the tiers (or levels) of the system has its own responsibilities.

A particular computer may not always be fixed in the role of client or server. That is, a computer may act as a server to a number of clients and yet act as a client to another server. For example, a web server maintaining a number of web pages may act as a *server* to clients running browsers. However, if the web server wants data from a relational database in order to satisfy some client request (for example, a list of products that are out of stock) then it acts as a *client* to a database server (see Figure 1). The request to the database server is usually expressed in the standard database query language SQL.

Another type of network architecture is known as a **peer-to-peer** (P2P) architecture because each computer has similar capabilities and responsibilities – each can act as a server as well as a client. Some P2P systems are hybrid in that they also have central computers that act only as servers, as shown in Figure 2.

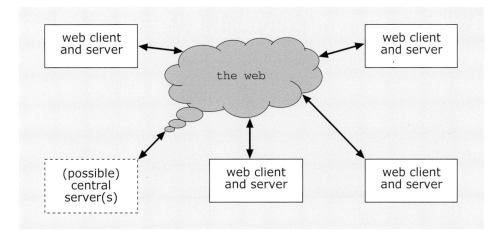

Figure 2   An example of a peer-to-peer architecture – hybrid P2P systems also use central servers for some functions

The P2P approach is used in many of the popular but controversial music-sharing systems. It is a robust approach in that it does not rely on one central server. It also makes it harder for hostile organizations to close down the system than it would be with a single-server system.

Both client–server and peer-to-peer architectures are widely used, and each has unique advantages and disadvantages. A full discussion of distributed system architecture is outside the scope of this course, so we will concentrate on client–server architectures.

You will find more details of distributed architectures in the course Developing concurrent distributed systems (M362).

SETI@home

An interesting example of a distributed system of a type that is gaining in popularity is the SETI@home system. This is part of the Search for Extra-Terrestrial Intelligence project, aimed at identifying life elsewhere in the universe by studying radio signals received on earth.

Participants can download client software, which runs on their PC instead of a screen saver. It thus uses otherwise 'unwanted' computer time to process radio signal data sent from a central server. The results are automatically returned to the server. In this way, the project can harness resources equivalent to a large supercomputer at greatly reduced cost.

This approach has now been adopted for a number of other applications, such as study of climate change, and for solving biological and genetic problems.

SAQ 2

What are the main potential difficulties with a distributed system such as the internet?

ANSWER..

Performance – the communication links between distant computers are much slower than the communication within a computer. It is very important to design a distributed system carefully to ensure good performance.

Security – unlike a system that is all in one location, it is normally difficult to physically secure all the components of a distributed system. Much communication typically takes place over shared public telecommunications links and the protocols used are publicly available.

3.3 Client–server computing on the internet

The internet contains a number of different kinds of servers. Some examples are as follows.

▶ *Web servers*. These hold web pages that are requested by clients running browsers.

▶ *Mail servers*. These store email messages that are intended for the users of the server and forward messages on to other mail servers.

▶ *FTP servers*. An FTP server uses the File Transfer Protocol to send stored files to FTP clients. When you download a music file from a website, or upload some web pages to update the contents of a website, you will normally be using FTP.

▶ *Print servers*. These are usually cheap PCs that manage access to one or more printers. They carry out the function of queuing requests for printing to the printers and informing clients that a particular print request has been completed.

▶ *Database servers*. These are servers that store large databases, and respond to queries about the data they hold.

SAQ 3

Give two examples of system architectures for distributed systems.

ANSWER..

One general approach to classifying architectures is the idea of *n*-tier architecture, where *n* can be 2, 3, 4 or more. Each tier has a particular responsibility.

Client–server systems are an example of a 2-tier architecture. Clients typically offer a user interface and some processing; servers offer a service to clients, such as providing web pages and perhaps also some processing.

A typical 3-tier architecture consists of a *database server* providing data from relational database tables, and a *web server* that formats this data into web pages and sends it to a *client* that provides the user interface for requesting and viewing data, typically using a browser.

A different approach to this is the peer-to-peer (P2P) architecture, where each host is more or less 'equal' and each can act as a server or a client.

Internet and web protocols

Although it can be quite straightforward to program access to internet and web resources in Java, it is useful to have some understanding of what is happening behind the scenes. In this section, we take a look at what goes on when you communicate across the internet – for example, to retrieve some information from a website.

4.1 Web servers

When you click on a web link to access a web page, you are actually sending a request to a web server. A **web server** is a program that sends back web pages in response to a request from a web client, typically a web browser program. More precisely, it sends the files associated with a web page: for example, files containing HTML text and files containing the graphics or other multimedia items for that web page.

Web servers are quite complicated pieces of software that carry out a number of functions. Some examples are as follows.

▶ They store web pages.

▶ They process requests for web pages, identify where they are stored and send them back together with an indication of what has been sent back.

▶ They carry out server-side processing, which may involve executing embedded Java code to dynamically update or construct web pages before they are sent to the requesting client. This is explained further in *Unit 10*.

▶ They enforce security policies specified by a webmaster.

▶ They cache web pages: that is, they store frequently accessed pages in fast memory so that they are dispensed quickly to clients.

▶ They generate log files that provide information about which clients requested which web pages. Such information is useful to the webmaster for maximizing performance and for marketing purposes.

4.2 Internet protocols

We have seen that the internet developed from research in the USA in the 1960s into robust networks that could survive attack by nuclear weapons. This has had an enormous influence on the way the internet works at a technical level – its distributed structure and what are known as the communication protocols.

A **protocol** is a set of rules that defines the details of how computers or other devices can communicate, so that both sides can understand the communication. The part of a protocol that asks for information is known as a **request**; the part that returns data is known as a **response**. A protocol can be thought of as a simple and restricted language that ensures that there is no ambiguity in the communications for both the requester and the respondent. We shall look at some specific examples of protocols later in this unit.

The early research led to two very important technologies that are still fundamental to the internet today – **packet switching** and the set of protocols known as **TCP/IP**. We discuss these technologies in more detail below.

The flexibility and resilience of the internet relies on packet switching – data is sent from one computer to other computers as a series of separate units called **packets**. For example, when you browse a web page the data that makes up that page is sent from the web server to the computer that requested it (the web client) as a series of data packets (see Figure 3).

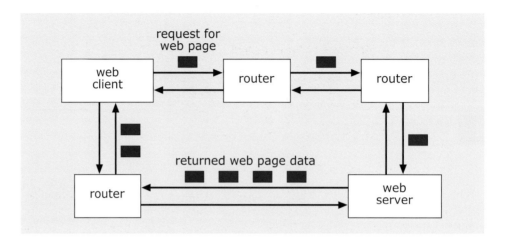

Figure 3   Packet switching – web server returning packets of data

A document or sizeable message to be sent across the internet is first split up into a number of fixed-size packets of data. Internet data is not usually sent directly from the sending computer to the receiving computer. Rather, it travels in a series of steps, normally with many intermediate computers or routing devices. The packet switching may involve sending packets by various different routes across the network to avoid any faulty or very busy parts of the system. This approach enables packets to reach their destination even if some communication lines are of poor quality or there are malfunctioning computers in the network. Of course, it may mean that packets do not all arrive in the same order that they were sent, so some reordering may need to happen at the receiver's end. Eventually all the packets received are reassembled in the correct order to produce the original document or message.

The fundamental set of protocols defining most communication across the internet is known as TCP/IP. This is made up of two distinct protocols – **Transmission Control Protocol (TCP)** and **Internet Protocol (IP)**. These define details of the packets of data sent and received, including their size in bits, the sequencing of packets and the meaning of each bit within a packet. The structures of IP and TCP packets are shown in Figure 4.

Figure 4 shows how each packet consists of some data together with a **packet header**, which contains details to direct the packet to its destination. You can think of the header information as the name and address on the envelope of a letter sent through the mail. The contents of the letter would be the data, in this case.

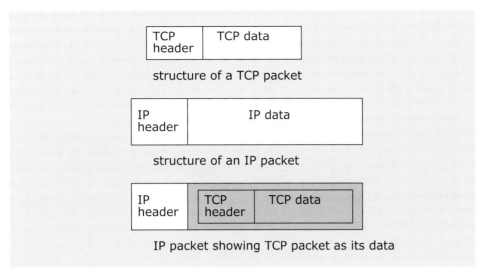

Figure 4   Structures of IP and TCP packets

Protocols in data communication are normally arranged in a series of **protocol levels** – the higher-level protocols assume that the lower-level protocols handle the lower-level details of the communication process. TCP is a higher-level protocol than IP – in fact, the 'data' in an IP packet is simply a TCP packet. IP is concerned with enabling individual packets to get from their source to a destination. IP packet headers are very simple, mainly containing the source and destination internet addresses.

TCP assumes that the IP protocol works most of the time but that some packets may get lost or corrupted in transit. Hence the TCP packet header specifies additional details, which ensure that any lost or erroneous packets are sent again and that packets can be reassembled into the correct order at the receiving end.

We shall see later that there are alternative protocols to TCP. However, all internet communication uses IP. TCP and IP are examples of **system protocols**, so called because they relate to the operation of the internet system, transferring data from one place to another, rather than to any particular use or application of the internet.

4.3   Application protocols

Internet applications make use of a large number of other protocols that operate at higher levels than TCP/IP. These are sometimes known as **application protocols** because they operate at the level of complete applications, like file transfer or web page access. Three examples are as follows.

▶   HTTP (HyperText Transfer Protocol) is used for communication between a client computer, using a browser, and a web server. It specifies, for example, which particular web page is required by the browser and it is used to return status information from the web server to indicate whether the page has been found.

▶   POP3 (Post Office Protocol version 3) is a simple protocol used for receipt of email from a computer known as a mail server. Elements of the protocol can be used to interrogate the server about how many email messages are currently being stored on the server or to communicate the reader's identity to the server.

▶   FTP (File Transfer Protocol) is used for the transfer of files of any type from one computer to another on the internet.

Activity 9.2
Sending an HTTP request.

HTTP (HyperText transfer protocol)

Web servers and browsers use HTTP to communicate with each other. Every request issued by a client browser gives rise to a response from the server. HTTP requests take the form of a command word, possibly followed by some additional information. The following example shows the use of the GET command to request a file called index. htm from a website:

    GET /index.htm HTTP/1.0

The file extension htm indicates that it is an HTML file. The 1.0 indicates that version 1.0 of HTTP is being used. The response to this request, if it is successful, will typically start as follows:

    HTTP/1.1 200 OK

This indicates that the server is using version 1.1 of HTTP (although it also understands version 1.0). The number 200 is a code to indicate (to a computer) that the request was successfully carried out and the text OK tells a human reader the same thing. This response is typically followed by other details, such as the date, time, details of the server, number of bytes sent and type of content returned (normally text and HTML). All these details are known as the *header information*. Finally, the contents of the requested file are sent to the browser, which normally displays them on the screen.

If the file requested is not present, or something else goes wrong, then the response will start with something different, such as:

    HTTP/1.1 404 Not Found

In this case, code 404 indicates to the browser software that the file was not found. The text Not Found is for users who may be directly reading the HTTP response.

Table 1 gives a summary of the most important HTTP commands and their functions. Full details of how to use these commands are outside the scope of this course but are well documented on the web.

Table 1 Some HTTP commands

HTTP command	Function
GET	retrieve data from a website (including header information)
HEAD	retrieve header information only from a website
OPTIONS	request list of available HTTP commands at a website
POST	send data to form a new document at a website
PUT	send data to update existing document at a website

SAQ 4

What is packet switching and why is it used for internet communication?

ANSWER...

Internet data travels in a series of steps from its source to its destination, normally with many intermediate computers or routing devices. With packet switching, the data is broken up into a series of separate small units called packets, and each packet is sent and received separately. Packets for a particular message may travel by different routes across the network.

The internet was designed to be robust and flexible – even if some of the network is faulty or missing, data should get through by an alternative route, if there are any such routes available. Packet switching allows packets of data to be re-routed or sent again, which is more efficient than resending an entire message.

4.4   Connections over the internet

There are two types of service that are provided on the internet. The first is a **connection-oriented service** where two computers establish a connection with each other before sending data – this is similar to establishing a voice telephone call before you start speaking. The connection is established by exchanging special packets of data in a process known as a **handshake**. When data is sent from one computer to another it usually passes via other computers in the internet, which are unaware of the fact that the sending and recipient computers have already established a connection.

The internet's connection-oriented service is mediated by TCP (Transmission Control Protocol). This protocol attempts to ensure that data always arrives in the correct order and in its entirety, even if some intervening computers are malfunctioning: it is a *reliable* protocol. The TCP handshake is a three-step process, which computers go through when negotiating a connection with one another. The first computer sends a special packet, the second computer sends a packet in reply and the first computer then acknowledges receipt of the reply. This establishes the connection.

The second type of service is known as a **connectionless service**. Here, there is no handshake between the computers that send and receive data, and there is no dialogue set up to ensure that all the data is received without errors. There are two consequences of this: the first is that data is sent very quickly; the second is that at times of high traffic, data may be lost or is likely to contain errors. For some applications, such as voice communication, this degradation may be acceptable if the degradation is not too severe. However, for applications where completely accurate data has to be received, a connectionless service is not used.

The part of the Internet Protocol set that implements connectionless data transfer is known as **User Datagram Protocol** (**UDP**), sometimes known as the Unreliable Data Protocol. Figure 5 shows that UDP packets (known as **datagrams**) are an alternative to TCP packets in forming the content of an IP packet. The UDP header is smaller and less detailed than the TCP header, reflecting the less sophisticated nature of UDP.

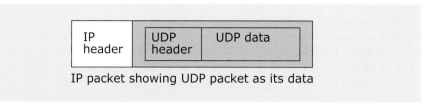

IP packet showing UDP packet as its data

Figure 5   Structure of a UDP packet (or datagram)

SAQ 5

What is the difference between a system protocol and an application protocol on the internet? How does this relate to the idea of levels of protocol?

ANSWER...

Protocols are the rules that govern how communication between devices takes place.

System protocols are at a relatively low level and they control data transfer that is applicable to many different uses of the internet – for example, most internet communication uses the TCP and IP system protocols to determine the detailed format and content of the packets sent.

Application protocols are those defined specifically to achieve a higher-level task such as transferring a file (FTP) or accessing a web page (HTTP). These are at a higher level of abstraction than system protocols. Application protocols make use of system protocols in their detailed implementation. For example, HTTP assumes the use of TCP to guarantee reliable transfer of data and TCP relies on IP for basic transfer of data packets. Therefore, from highest to lowest level these protocols are HTTP, TCP and then IP.

5 Addressing on the internet

In order to send data to a computer over a network such as the internet you need to be able to identify the computer uniquely by its address. There are two ways of identifying a host on the internet, using a **symbolic address** or a **numeric address**.

5.1 Symbolic addressing

The most familiar form of addressing is symbolic. This is the sort of web address you see on an advertisement, and which you typically enter into a browser to access a particular site. It uses a form of hierarchical naming that identifies a decreasing collection of computers at each level, finally ending up with a single computer. For example, consider the following symbolic address for the main Open University web server:

`www.open.ac.uk`

To interpret this address you read it from right to left:

`uk` signifies a collection of computers associated with the United Kingdom;

`ac` identifies those computers associated with academic institutions such as universities;

`open` refers to those computers associated with The Open University;

`www` is the name of a computer, the name usually given to a web server.

Thus the address can be read as:

The computer `www` belonging to The Open University, an academic institution associated with the United Kingdom.

There are many other collections of computers within the internet – for example, the collection `com` is associated with companies. So, for example, the address:

`www.google.com`

refers to the computer `www` associated with the company `google`, which is a commercial company offering a well-known internet search engine.

5.2 IP addressing

Underlying the symbolic addressing that users find convenient and memorable, the internet systems actually use numbers to identify each computer. A numeric address (or **IP address**) typically uses a set of four numbers separated by dots. For example:

`193.22.33.201`

Remember that IP means Internet Protocol.

This form of address uniquely identifies a computer by these four numbers. Each number fits into 8 bits (so that each number must be in the range 0 to 255) making 32 bits in total. It is often known as **dotted quad notation** or IP Version 4 (IPv4) addressing.

IP version 6 addressing

Owing to the huge number of people now using the internet, there are not enough IPv4 addresses available to meet the expected future demand – 32 bits allow 4.2 billion addresses, in theory, although less in practice because of the way addresses are allocated in blocks to particular users. So a new version of IP addressing, IP Version 6 (IPv6) is being introduced. IPv6 uses 128 bits in total, allowing 3×10^{38} addresses. This works out at 6×10^{23} addresses for every square metre on the planet, so it should be quite a while before these addresses are all allocated!

5.3   The Internet Domain Name Service

The part of the internet that keeps track of which computers are associated with which symbolic addresses is known as the **Internet Domain Name Service**, usually abbreviated to **DNS**.

Whenever access is made to the internet – for example, when sending an email to someone whose mail server is located at a particular computer – the DNS is consulted to find out the IP address corresponding to the symbolic name. Strictly speaking, it finds the IP address corresponding to the **domain name**, the part of the symbolic name associated with a particular organization, such as google.com or open.ac.uk. The DNS is one of the most heavily used parts of the internet. It is actually provided by a number of collaborating servers throughout the internet.

Activity 9.3
Ping-ing a website.

The DNS is a specific example of a type of service known as a **name service**. Such a service maintains details of resources in a system and their symbolic names; with the DNS, the resources are individual computers on the internet that are associated with symbolic names. Other name services keep and maintain data on other resources such as users, printers or security policies.

5.4   Ports and sockets

An important concept in the TCP and UDP protocols is that of a **port**. A port is a conduit into a host on the internet. In this context, a port is a *logical idea* – it is not the same as a parallel port or a USB port, which are actual pieces of hardware to which you can connect wires.

TCP communication into and out of a computer is via numbered ports. Ports numbered from 0 to 1023 are reserved for dedicated services. For example, port 80 is used for web server communication, port 21 is used for FTP requests and port 110 for POP3 email communication. This allows a client to request a particular kind of service and allows servers to *listen* for particular kinds of requests on specific port numbers (see Figure 6).

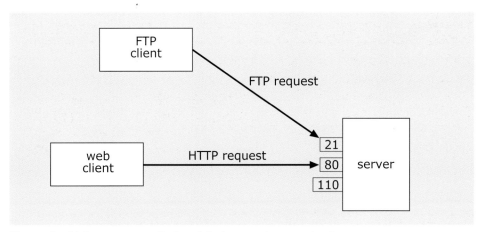

Figure 6   Using ports to distinguish the service required

If you are writing Java programs that use ports then you should avoid using ports in this dedicated range, unless you intend to use one of these services. UDP communication also uses numbered ports. The maximum port number for both TCP and UDP is 65534 (as this fits into the 16-bit slots reserved for port numbers in the packet header).

A **socket** is the software mechanism that allows programs to transfer data across the internet using TCP/IP. A socket object in Java is associated with a port number and the address of a host, specified either as an IP address or in symbolic form. For client–server communication, we need a matching pair of sockets, one on the client and the other on the server. We will show how we program this later in the unit.

SAQ 6

What does the DNS do and why is it needed?

ANSWER   ....

DNS stands for Internet Domain Name Service. Computers on the internet are individually identified by means of a numeric IP address (in IPv4, this is dotted quad notation, for example, `198.23.200.16`). This is hard for human users to remember, so symbolic domain names, such as `open.ac.uk`, are used instead. The DNS is used to find the IP address corresponding to a symbolic address entered by users. This allows messages to be sent to the required destination.

5.5   Addressing resources on the web

Resources on the web are identified using unique addresses. This unique address is known as a **Uniform Resource Locator**, usually abbreviated to **URL**. The first part of the URL indicates the protocol to be used in accessing the resource and the second part indicates the address where the resource can be found. An example of this is shown below:

```
http://www.open.ac.uk/Computing/Staff/I_Newton.htm
```

Here, `http` specifies that the resource is a web page and so the protocol to use is HTTP. The part after the first two slashes provides the name of the host computer, `www.open.ac.uk`. The remainder of the URL is known as the path and it specifies the route to the resource. In this case, it can be found in the folder `Staff`, a subfolder of `Computing`. The name of the file is `I_Newton.htm` and the file extension `htm` indicates that it is an HTML file.

All web resources are referenced using this convention. In this course, we shall concentrate on web pages; however, you should be aware that there are other forms of URL using different protocols, such as FTP for file transfer. For example:

```
ftp://www.open.ac.uk/Computing/downloads/stuff.doc
```

would indicate the location of a (mythical) file that could be downloaded from the Open University website. A file located on the local computer system would have a URL with the protocol part `file`. For example:

```
file://C:/Computing/Staff/I_Newton.htm
```

This indicates to the browser that it can locate the file simply by looking in the specified folder on drive `C:` of the local system, and does not have to access it using a protocol such as HTTP.

The `URL` class that we saw in Section 2 has a number of constructors that allow the programmer to create URLs. The simple constructor that we saw earlier is the single argument constructor that creates a URL from its string description. For example:

```
URL openUniversity = new URL("http://www.open.ac.uk");
```

Alternatively, it is possible to set the various components of the URL individually:

```
URL openUniversity = new URL("http", "www.open.ac.uk", "");
```

Here the arguments represent the protocol, the host (that is, the computer name) and the path. Where the path is left empty, as in this example, the URL refers to the home page for this host.

It is also possible to specify the port to be used, as in the following example of invoking the URL constructor:

```
URL open = new URL("ftp", "ftp.open.ac.uk", 25, "/staff.txt");
```

This creates the URL corresponding to `ftp://ftp.open.ac.uk:25/staff.txt`, which can be used for FTP access to the file `staff.txt` on port `25` (if the FTP server is set up to permit use of this non-standard port for FTP). Note that the port number must be specified as an integer and that the path must start with a forward slash as shown.

Most of the methods within the `URL` class get or set the various components of the URL. For example, they can return the protocol or the host parts of the URL:

```
String protocol = openUniversity.getProtocol();
String hostName = openUniversity.getHost();
if (protocol.equals("http"))
{
    ...
```

In general, the getter methods for the `URL` class are more useful than the setter methods. Once a `URL` object has been constructed you will seldom want to change it, although you may want to change the contents of the resource to which it refers.

SAQ 7

(a) Explain the components of the following URL:

`http://intra.mkt.edu/physics/energy/bubble.jpg`

(b) Is the following URL correctly formed? If not, indicate how you would correct it.

`ftp://www/englit/documents/`

ANSWERS ....

(a) This URL can be broken down as follows. The path is `/physics/energy/bubble.jpg`, the host is `intra.mkt.edu` and the protocol part is `http`. This represents a file called `bubble.jpg` (presumably an image, compressed in JPEG format) that is stored in the `physics` folder, subfolder `energy` on the computer called `intra`, located in domain `mkt.edu`. (`edu` is commonly used in the USA for educational institutions such as universities – the rest of the world is normally more modest, but then the USA got there first.) The protocol component, `http`, indicates that the resource can be accessed using HTTP, which defines communication over the web.

(b) No, it is not a valid URL. It omits the domain name where presumably the computer `www` is located. Note also that it specifies only a folder called `documents`, not the file within that folder that is required – this is permissible in some URLs where there is a default filename to access. The protocol `ftp` is correct – this indicates that the File Transfer Protocol is to be used. So a correct, full URL might look like this:

`ftp://www.open.ac.uk/englit/documents/A254.doc`

On the other hand, the UK is the only country in the world that does not have to display its name on its postage stamps – because the UK got there first.

URI versus URL

In this text we have used the term URL, for Uniform Resource Locator, to indicate the location on the web of various resources such as a web page, a video clip or an FTP site.

You may also come across the term URI for Uniform Resource Identifier. This is a related and more general term than URL, and some authors may use it in preference to the term URL. A URI is intended to be a generic name for any of a class of ways of identifying resources on the internet. Two types of URI that have been proposed are URL (as we have seen) and URN (Uniform Resource Name). The idea of a URI is that it is a unique name that is used to access the resource. It is not necessarily a specific file location (it may be a call to an application or a database, for example). If it is a specific file location, then it is a URL.

At the time of writing, implementations of URNs are not widespread; only URLs are in common use. So for most practical purposes at present, the terms URI and URL mean the same thing.

By definition, all URLs are URIs.

Not all URIs are URLs, but at present almost all URIs in use are URLs.

6 Programming with sockets

Earlier we introduced the notion of a socket as a software mechanism that allows the transfer of data between programs. A socket is a logical idea of a connection to a host on the internet, and each socket is unique since it consists of an IP address and a port number.

6.1 Sockets on the client

The class `Socket` allows us to create sockets on the client system. The most common `Socket` constructor has the form:

```
Socket(String, int)
```

This creates a `Socket` object that allows communication with the computer, which has the address given by the first argument, using the port given by the second argument. For example, consider the following code:

```
Socket sock = new Socket("catalogue.acme.co.uk", 4000);
```

This creates a `Socket` object to link to port `4000` on the `catalogue` computer associated with the domain `acme.co.uk`. You can also use numeric IP addressing (dotted quad notation) for this address, as follows:

```
Socket sock = new Socket("199.200.34.123", 4000);
```

Communication between clients and a server is achieved by input/output streams. Each socket has an associated input stream and output stream – the methods `getInputStream` and `getOutputStream` give access to these streams. For example:

```
Socket sock = new Socket("catalogue.acme.co.uk", 4000);
InputStream is = sock.getInputStream();
OutputStream os = sock.getOutputStream();
...
```

These streams can then be used to send and receive data, using a similar approach to writing and reading files. In order to show how this happens, Section 7 gives a detailed example.

6.2 Sockets on the server

On the server system we also need a socket for each connection to a client. However, creation of sockets must be approached a little differently. This is because the server does not normally initiate a connection – rather, it waits for a client to request a connection. Hence it cannot create a socket until it knows the address of the client that wants to establish a connection.

The key class for dealing with this is the `ServerSocket` class. This is used within a server for setting up sockets that are to be associated with a client. The class has two important constructors. The first has the form:

```
ServerSocket(int)
```

This sets up a `ServerSocket` object associated with a particular port specified by its single argument. As you will see below, this object is then used to create the sockets that are associated with clients communicating with the server via that port. For example, the following code causes the server to 'listen' on port 80 (normally used for HTTP requests).

```
ServerSocket ss = new ServerSocket(80);
```

In practice, this means that the server checks incoming TCP packets to see whether they are addressed to port 80.

The second constructor is defined by:

```
ServerSocket(int, int)
```

The first argument is the port to be used, as before. The second argument is the maximum number of clients allowed to wait for connections from the server. For example, the code:

```
ServerSocket ss = new ServerSocket(3000, 30);
```

sets up the `ServerSocket` object referenced by `ss`, which is associated with port 3000 and with a client queue of maximum length 30. If, while processing a request from a client, another client attempts to access the service via this port, then the new client connection request will be placed in the queue and will be dealt with after the first client's connection has terminated. If the queue is full, any further client connections will be refused.

Once a `ServerSocket` object is created, the server will wait for clients to request a connection. When a connection is made, a socket linked to the client is created; this is achieved via the `accept` method.

An example of its use is shown below:

```
// server code
ServerSocket ss = new ServerSocket(3000, 30);
...
// wait until connection request made by client
Socket sock = ss.accept();
```

When the `accept` method is first executed, it is blocked: it stops running until a client attempts to create a socket on the port associated with the `ServerSocket` object. The `accept` method creates a socket that links to the client requesting the service provided on port 3000 by the server. This socket can then be used to access input and output streams in the same way as we saw above on the client (see Figure 7).

Activity 9.4
Accessing a server using Telnet.

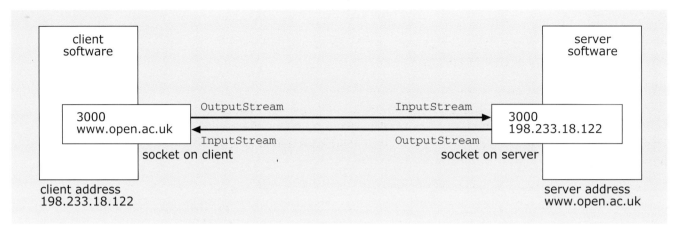

Figure 7   Client–server link on port 3000 using TCP sockets

In programming servers and clients you should bear in mind that:

▶ a connection is a linked pair of sockets (see Figure 7);

▶ at the server end, the socket has the address of the client and a suitable port number for the service required by the client;

▶ at the client end, the socket has the address of the server and the same port number as the server for the particular service required;

▶ the InputStream entering the client receives data from the OutputStream leaving the server and the InputStream entering the server receives data from the OutputStream leaving the client.

The FTP protocol

The FTP or *file transfer protocol* was defined early in the history of the internet, but is still in widespread use. When you download a music file from a website, or upload some web pages to update the contents of a website, you will normally be using FTP.

FTP uses two TCP connections – so there are two separate ports at the server and two separate ports at the client. One connection is for handling control information (normally port 21 at both the client and the server) and the other is for transferring the data (normally port 20 at each end). So the illustration in Figure 6 is correct in showing requests directed to port 21, but does not show the whole story.

Along the control connection (port 21), the FTP client sends special command words in the form specified by FTP, such as:

USER   supplies the user name (often 'anonymous' for free access)

PASS   supplies the password, if needed, for access to the server

RETR   retrieves contents of a specified file

QUIT   terminates the connections

The FTP server responds on port 21, indicating whether or not the request was successful.

In response to a successful RETR command, the server will send the file data on the data connection (port 20). This is different from HTTP, which we saw earlier, in that HTTP sends control information and data along the same connection (normally port 80).

SAQ 8

Why does a `ServerSocket` have only an associated port number, whereas a `Socket` has both a port number and an IP address?

ANSWER...

When client software creates a socket using the `Socket` class, it must know both the server computer with which it will be communicating and the port number to be used. This ensures that data goes to and from the correct IP address and is directed to the appropriate service.

The `ServerSocket` specifies only a port number on which a service is offered. This service may be requested by any one or more of many different client computers, and we normally do not know the addresses of these clients in advance. So it would not make sense to specify an IP address for a particular client when the `ServerSocket` object is created. When a particular client requests a connection to the server, the `accept` method of the `ServerSocket` object is used to create a new `Socket` object on the server. This `Socket` object has the client's IP address as well as the port number and so it can communicate with the corresponding socket on the client.

7 A simple client–server example

To illustrate the ideas discussed in the previous section, we now consider a very simple example of a client communicating with a server. In this case, the client connects to the server and receives a single message, which it displays on screen. Both the client and the server then terminate. The client does not send any messages to the server.

In a more realistic interaction, there would be a two-way communication: the client would be able to send any number of messages containing requests to the server and the server would respond appropriately to those requests. The server would keep running until it was explicitly closed down. It would be useful if the server could deal with requests from a number of different clients.

These more complex scenarios will be discussed in later sections. For now, we consider only the case of one client receiving a single message from the server. We start by looking at the code for the server.

7.1 Simple server

We define a class for the server called `HelloServer`. This has a number of instance variables concerned with the sockets and streams needed for the client and server to communicate. The first part of the class, including the constructor, is shown below. For clarity, we will defer explanations of some of the instance variables at this stage – these will be discussed when we look at the methods of this class later in this section.

```java
public class HelloServer
{
    private ServerSocket serverSocket;
    private Socket socket;  // socket to link to the client

    // streams for communication to client
    private OutputStream os;
    private PrintWriter toClient;

    // use a high numbered non-dedicated port
    static final int PORT_NUMBER = 3000;
    static final String MESSAGE_TO_CLIENT = "Hello Walrus";

    // constructor
    public HelloServer ()
    {
        try
        {
            // create a ServerSocket object to listen on the port
            serverSocket = new ServerSocket(PORT_NUMBER);
        }
```

```
        catch (IOException e)
        {
            System.out.println("Trouble on port " +
                              PORT_NUMBER + ": " + e);
        }
    } // end constructor
    ...
```

The constructor does only one thing – it creates a `ServerSocket` object, which will permit the server to listen on the specified port waiting for a client to attempt to make a connection. In this case we use port `3000`, but there is nothing special about this number except that it is out of the range 0–1023 dedicated to standard services. The constructor for a `ServerSocket` object can generate an `IOException`, so we provide code to catch and report this.

The main work of the server is carried out by the `run` method, as follows:

```
public void run ()
{
    try
    {
        // wait for a connection request
        socket = serverSocket.accept();
        openStreams();
        toClient.println(MESSAGE_TO_CLIENT);
        closeStreams();
        socket.close();
    }
    catch (IOException e)
    {
        System.out.println("Trouble with a connection " + e);
    }
}
```

Here, the `accept` method of the `ServerSocket` object causes the server to wait until a client attempts to make a connection. This attempt occurs when the client software creates a socket on the client computer. When a client does attempt to make a connection, a socket is created at the server and a reference to this new socket is stored in the instance variable `socket`. Next, we must use the private method `openStreams` to open the streams that allow the server to send a message to the client. This gives us the situation of two linked sockets – one on the client and one on the server – as illustrated in Figure 7 in Subsection 6.2.

We then send a message to the client using the `PrintWriter` object referenced by `toClient`. Finally, we close the streams using the private method `closeStreams` and also close the socket to terminate the connection to the client.

We can take a closer look at the private methods, starting with `openStreams`, as follows:

```
// set up streams for communicating with the client
private void openStreams() throws IOException
{
    final boolean AUTO_FLUSH = true;
    os = socket.getOutputStream();
    toClient = new PrintWriter(os, AUTO_FLUSH);
}
```

We use the getOutputStream method of the Socket object to obtain the OutputStream that will enable us to send output to the client. We use the OutputStream object referenced by the instance variable os to create a PrintWriter object referenced by toClient. Essentially, the PrintWriter object wraps around the OutputStream object, and offers a more convenient way to send data using the println method. This PrintWriter object is defined to be autoflushed: that is, the output will be sent immediately after execution of a println method, rather than being held in a buffer.

When we have finished with these output streams, it is important to close them and this is the role of the closeStreams method, whose code is as follows:

```
// close output streams to client
private void closeStreams () throws IOException
{
    toClient.close();
    os.close();
}
```

Both of these methods, openStreams and closeStreams, can give rise to an IOException. Since they do not handle the exception within the method, it must be declared in the method header. The exception will then be handled by the code in the try-catch statement of the run method that invokes these two helper methods.

This completes the code for the simple server, except that in order to run the server we must have a main method and this is located in a separate class, TestHelloServer, as follows:

```
public class TestHelloServer
{
    // create a server and have it greet the client
    public static void main (String[] args)
    {
        HelloServer server1 = new HelloServer();
        server1.run();
    }
}
```

Activity 9.5
Testing the simple server.

The main method creates a HelloServer object and invokes its run method. Until we have a client to interact with this server, this causes the server to wait when it reaches the accept method invocation on the ServerSocket object. In Subsection 7.2, we shall see how to write the code for the client that can rescue this server from its lonely wait.

7.2 Simple client

We define a class, called HelloClient, for the client. As for the server, this has a number of instance variables relating to the sockets and streams that are needed to enable the client to communicate with the server. In this simple client we do not define a constructor, as there is nothing for it to do. The main work of the class, as in the server, is in a method called run.

The code for the first part of the class, including the `run` method, is as follows:

```
public class HelloClient
{
    // streams used for communicating with server
    private InputStream is;
    private BufferedReader fromServer;
    private Socket socket;  // socket to server

    // use local host address for server
    static final String SERVER_ADDRESS = "127.0.0.1";
    static final int SERVER_PORT_NUMBER = 3000;

    public void run ()
    {
        // set up connection to the server
        try
        {
            socket = new Socket(SERVER_ADDRESS, SERVER_PORT_NUMBER);
            openStreams();

            String messageFromServer = fromServer.readLine();
            System.out.println("Server said: " + messageFromServer);

            closeStreams();
            socket.close();
        }
        catch (IOException e)
        {
            System.out.println("Trouble contacting the server " + e);
        }
    }
```

The code in the `run` method carries out all the functions of this simple client with the aid of two helper methods, `openStreams` and `closeStreams`. First, it creates a `Socket` object that connects to a specified port at a specified server address. In this example, we use port `3000` again, as this is the port number expected by the simple server. The above code uses the special IP address "`127.0.0.1`", known as the **loopback address** or the **local host** because it indicates that we want to communicate with a server on the same computer as the client. To communicate with any other computer you can simply change the value of the constant called `SERVER_ADDRESS` to either the symbolic name or the IP address of the other computer.

Once the socket has been created and the connection established (this is the job of the `accept` method of the `ServerSocket` object in the server software above) we can go on to open the streams that are needed for communicating with the server. If anything goes wrong at this stage (for example, if the server software is not running) this will normally give rise to an `IOException`, which will be caught and handled by the `catch` block.

The `openStreams` method creates a `BufferedReader` object, referenced by the `fromServer` instance variable, for text input from the server. We then use the `readLine` method to obtain a line of message text from the server, and this message is displayed on the screen. Finally, we close the streams using the private method `closeStreams` and also close the socket, to terminate the connection to the server.

As with the server, the private helper methods are quite straightforward. We start with openStreams, as follows:

```
// open streams for communicating with the server
private void openStreams () throws IOException
{
    is = socket.getInputStream();
    fromServer = new BufferedReader(new InputStreamReader(is));
}
```

We use the getInputStream method of the Socket object to enable us to get input from the server. We use the InputStream object referenced by the instance variable is to create a BufferedReader object referenced by fromServer. Again, the reason for this layering or wrapping of streams is that a BufferedReader has more convenient ways to read data than the lower-level InputStream. For example, we can use the readLine method to read text input.

When we have finished with these input streams, it is important to close them and this is the role of the closeStreams method, whose code is as follows:

```
// close streams to server
private void closeStreams () throws IOException
{
    fromServer.close();
    is.close();
}
```

As with the corresponding methods in the server class both of these methods, openStreams and closeStreams, can give rise to an IOException. This is declared in the method header and is handled by the code in the run method.

The client code is run by a main method located in the separate class, TestHelloClient, as follows:

```
public class TestHelloClient
{
    public static void main (String[] args)
    {
        HelloClient client1 = new HelloClient();
        client1.run();
    }
}
```

Activity 9.6
Putting the simple client and server together.

Before running the client, you need to start the corresponding server. Otherwise, an exception will occur when the client tries to create a socket linked to the server. When the client and server above run successfully, the client should produce the following output:

```
Server said: Hello Walrus
```

After this, the client and server both close their respective ends of the connection and terminate.

8 A name service

In the previous section, we saw how to code a simple server and a simple client. We will now show how we program a more complex client–server system that implements a name service.

A name service provides information about a resource, given the symbolic name of that resource. For example, a name service might keep information about printer names that could then be used to obtain the characteristics of a printer, such as its type, its manufacturer and its speed. The example that we describe here is a name service that returns the email addresses of employees of a company when given their names. For example, the user `Egbert Dreistein` would be associated with his email address `E. A.Dreistein@open.ac.uk`.

The name server will run continuously, accepting a series of requests from one or more clients. It can, however, deal with only one client at any given time – if the server is connected to a client, then any other client requesting to connect will be queued until the first client connection has been closed. The client has a graphical user interface (GUI) to allow the user to input requests and view responses. One of the possible client requests is a message to inform the server that the client is terminating the connection. This allows the server to close the connection to this client and proceed to serve the next client, if any.

First, we will develop the code for the server. In this example, the data is stored in a `HashMap` object that maps user names to email addresses. In practice, some file-based medium such as a relational database would normally be used.

8.1 The server code

The server is implemented by the class `NameServer`, which has a constructor and several methods, only one of which is public. Most of the structure of the server is in the public method, `run`, but first we look at the instance variable declarations and the constructor. The start of the class definition is as follows:

```
public class NameServer
{
    private HashMap nameDatabase;
    private ServerSocket ss;
    private Socket socket;

    // streams for connections
    private InputStream is;
    private OutputStream os;

    // writer and reader for communication
    private PrintWriter toClient;
    private BufferedReader fromClient;

    // use a high numbered non-dedicated port
    static final int PORT_NUMBER = 3000;
```

```
// protocol definitions
// sent by client:
static final String CLIENT_QUITTING = "Exit";

// sent by server
static final String USER_NOT_FOUND = "User not known";

// constructor
public NameServer ()
{
    nameDatabase = setUpNameDatabase();

    // establish a ServerSocket
    try
    {
        ss = new ServerSocket(PORT_NUMBER);
    }
    catch (Exception e)
    {
        System.out.println("Trouble with ServerSocket,
                          port " + PORT_NUMBER + ": " + e);
    }
} // end constructor
...
```

The instance variables are mostly similar to those we saw in the simple server in Subsection 7.1. They include variables that reference `ServerSocket` and `Socket` objects as well as variables that reference streams for communication with the client. In this case, since the communication is two-way, we have streams for reading input from the client as well as the streams for output that we saw in the previous server.

The constructor does two things only. It sets up the database of information that associates users' names with their email addresses. It also creates a `ServerSocket` object, to enable the server to listen on the specified port. As before, we have used port `3000`, but this has no special significance apart from being outside the reserved range for dedicated ports.

The name database is stored in a `HashMap` object which, as we saw in *Unit 5*, implements a hash table to store key–value pairs. This will allow the server to quickly look up the email address associated with a given user name. The `HashMap` object is created by a private helper method, `setUpNameDatabase`, as follows:

```
// set up name database and add sample data
private HashMap <String, String> setUpNameDatabase ()
{
    HashMap <String, String> db = new HashMap <String, String>();

    db.put("Gareth Williams", "G.R.Williams@java2.co.uk");
    db.put("Robert Thomas", "R.Thomas@java2.co.uk");
    db.put("William Wilson", "W.Wilson@java2.co.uk");
    db.put("Anne Land", "A.Land@java2.co.uk");
    db.put("Dave Phillips", "D.Phillips@java2.co.uk");
    db.put("Kirsten Davis", "K.L.Davis@java2.co.uk");

    return db;
}
```

Most of the work for this server is carried out by the `run` method, with the help of a number of private methods, as follows:

```
public void run ()
{
    try
    {
        // loop endlessly waiting for client connections
        while (true)
        {
            // wait for a connection request
            socket = ss.accept();
            openStreams();
            processClientRequests();
            closeStreams();
            socket.close();
        }
    }
    catch (IOException e)
    {
        System.out.println("Trouble with a connection " + e);
    }
}
```

The basic structure of the server is a continuous loop containing code that causes the server to wait for a client to connect and then to process any requests from that client. When the client has no further requests, the connection is closed and the server returns to wait for any further clients to connect.

When a client succeeds in connecting, the `accept` method returns a `Socket` object that allows communication with the client. The helper method `openStreams` opens the necessary streams for input from and output to the client, and then the method `processClientRequests` repeatedly processes client requests. When the client sends a message indicating that it wishes to terminate the connection, the streams are closed by the helper method `closeStreams` and, finally, the connection to this client is closed by invoking the `close` method of the `Socket` object. The server then returns to the start of the loop to wait for another client to connect.

This structure is typical for servers, regardless of the precise service being offered. The content of the helper method `processClientRequests` can be adjusted to suit the particular service that is needed and the protocol for the communication.

Note also the `try-catch` construct, which handles any `IOException` objects thrown by code in the `run` method or any of its helper methods.

We will now look at the code for each of the remaining helper methods, to see in more detail how the server works.

The `openStreams` and `closeStreams` methods are similar to the corresponding methods in the simple server in Subsection 7.1. The main difference is that we need to deal with streams for text input from the client as well as the output streams we saw in the previous server example. The code for `openStreams` is as follows:

```
// set up streams for communicating with the client
private void openStreams () throws IOException
{
    final boolean AUTO_FLUSH = true;
    is = socket.getInputStream();
    fromClient = new BufferedReader(new InputStreamReader(is));
    os = socket.getOutputStream();
    toClient = new PrintWriter(os, AUTO_FLUSH);
}
```

All the variables used here to reference the various streams are instance variables. This is because we will need to use them in a number of other methods of this class.

The next helper method, `processClientRequests`, carries out the key work of the server – reading client requests and responding to them. The structure is simple and typical of servers: the server repeatedly reads a client request string using the `readLine` method of the `BufferedReader` class. In this case, the request is simply the name of a user, and the processing involves looking up this name in the hash table that stores the name database. If the name is found, then the `get` method of the `HashMap` object will return a string corresponding to the email address of the user; this string is sent as the reply to the client. If there is no matching name in the database, the `get` method will return a null reference and the server sends a suitable reply (in this case 'User not known') to the client. The method then waits for further requests from the client and processes them repeatedly until the special request string is read, indicating that the client is closing down. The method then terminates. The code is as follows:

```
private void processClientRequests () throws IOException
{
    String userName; // name request from client
    String userEmail;
    String reply;  // reply sent to client
    // get request from client
    userName = fromClient.readLine();
    while (!(userName.equals(CLIENT_QUITTING)))
    {
        userEmail = (String) nameDatabase.get(userName);
        if (userEmail == null)
        {
            reply = USER_NOT_FOUND;
        }
        else
        {
            reply = userEmail;
        }
        // send reply to client
        toClient.println(reply);
        // get next request
        userName = fromClient.readLine();
    }
}
```

Again, note that this method may generate an `IOException`: for example, if the connection became faulty while trying to input or output messages. Such an exception would be handled in the `run` method.

When all requests from a particular client have been processed, the `closeStreams` method closes down the streams between the server and this particular client, as follows:

```
private void closeStreams () throws IOException
{
    toClient.close();
    os.close();
    fromClient.close();
    is.close();
}
```

Execution in the main loop of the `run` method then returns to the `accept` method, as in the following extract from the method code shown earlier:

```
...
// loop endlessly waiting for client connections
while (true)
{
    // wait for a connection request
    socket = ss.accept();
...
```

Again the server waits for a client to connect and then proceeds to open streams, processes requests and eventually closes the connection for this client also. The server continues to run like this indefinitely, as this server has no way of receiving a shutdown command for the server itself. To stop this server you must close down the program, using whatever facilities the environment provides to terminate the programs.

Finally, note the approach that is used for exception handling. Several of the helper methods may generate an `IOException`; this is declared in the headers of these methods and the exception is handled by a single `try-catch` construct in the `run` method. An alternative approach would be to have a `try-catch` construct within each of the helper methods and to deal with each exception locally within the method where it occurs. This has some potential advantages if we want to take different recovery or reporting actions for the various possible locations of the exception. However, in this simple example we just want to report the exception and terminate the program, so the same action is appropriate for all occurrences of the exception.

The only other thing required is a class containing a `main` method, which can be used to create and run the `NameServer` object. A suitable class, called `TestNameServer`, is as follows:

```
public class TestNameServer
{
    // create a name server to respond to client requests
    public static void main (String[] args)
    {
        NameServer server1 = new NameServer();
        server1.run();
    } // end main
}
```

The `main` method creates a `NameServer` object and invokes its `run` method. This causes the server to set up the name database and then to wait for a suitable client to connect. Next, we shall discuss how we write just such a client.

Activity 9.7
Testing the name server.

8.2 The client code

This section describes the client code for the name service. The client user interface consists of a single window, containing two labelled text fields and two buttons, as shown in Figure 8.

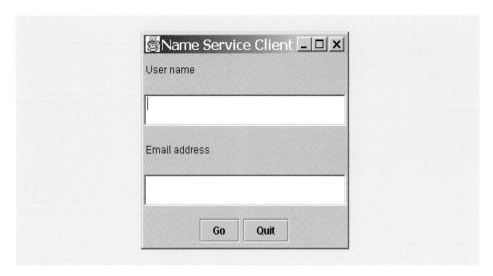

Figure 8   The client user interface window

The Go button sends the employee's user name in the first text field to the server. When the server replies with the email address of the user, this is displayed in the second text field. The Quit button disconnects the client from the server and closes the client.

The client class is declared as follows:

```
public class NameClient extends JFrame implements ActionListener
{
    ...
```

This means that the NameClient class is a kind of frame; it inherits from the JFrame class provided by the Swing library of user interface classes. It also implements the interface ActionListener – this ensures that the client window responds to events such as clicking on one of the buttons.

The constructor is quite simple – it has three tasks, as shown below:

```
public NameClient (String title)
{
    super(title);
    setUpGUI();
    connectToServer();
}
```

First, it invokes the constructor for its superclass (in this case, JFrame) – this sets the window title. Using two private helper methods, it constructs the graphical interface (as shown in Figure 8) and then connects to the name server, whose code we looked at in Subsection 8.1. Once a client object has been created by executing this constructor, it simply waits for the user to click on one of the buttons before responding. This is what we defined as event-driven programming – the button click events drive the client system.

The detailed code for setting up the GUI is as follows:

```
// set up client graphical user interface
private void setUpGUI ()
{
    final int CLIENT_WINDOW_WIDTH = 260;
    final int CLIENT_WINDOW_HEIGHT = 250;
    final int TEXTFIELD_WIDTH = 20;

    userName = new TextField(TEXTFIELD_WIDTH);
    userEmailAddress = new TextField(TEXTFIELD_WIDTH);
    goButton = new JButton("Go");
    quitButton = new JButton("Quit");

    Container content = getContentPane();
    content.setLayout(new GridLayout(5, 1));

    content.add(new Label("User name"));
    content.add(userName);
    content.add(new Label("Email address"));
    content.add(userEmailAddress);

    JPanel buttonPanel = new JPanel();
    buttonPanel.add(goButton);
    buttonPanel.add(quitButton);
    content.add(buttonPanel);

    // register button listeners
    goButton.addActionListener(this);
    quitButton.addActionListener(this);

    setSize(CLIENT_WINDOW_WIDTH, CLIENT_WINDOW_HEIGHT);
    setVisible(true);
}
```

This follows the standard pattern of creating a number of user interface objects – text fields, buttons and labels – and adding these to the frame using a suitable layout. In this case, the frame layout manager is a simple `GridLayout`, but other more complex layouts would be possible. Finally, the client frame object is registered as a listener for both the buttons. This means that the `NameClient` class must provide a method that responds to any button clicks – more details of this are given later in this section.

The code for connecting to the server is in the helper method `connectToServer`. This creates a socket and then opens the streams for communication with the server:

```
// set up connection to the server
private void connectToServer ()
{
    try
    {
        socket = new Socket(SERVER_ADDRESS, SERVER_PORT_NUMBER);
        openStreams();
    }
    catch (IOException e)
    {
        System.out.println("Trouble contacting the server " + e);
    }
}
```

The socket that is created here and referenced by the instance variable `socket` is associated with the address of the server as well as the port number, which must be the same as the port number used in the server code. Either the IP address or the symbolic form of the server address can be used. This method also invokes the `openStreams` method, which is very similar to the corresponding methods we have seen previously. Any exceptions that occur are handled within the `connectToServer` method. The code for the method `openStreams` is as follows:

```
// open streams for input and output
    private void openStreams () throws IOException
    {
        final boolean AUTO_FLUSH = true;
        is = socket.getInputStream();
        fromServer = new BufferedReader(new InputStreamReader(is));
        os = socket.getOutputStream();
        toServer = new PrintWriter(os, AUTO_FLUSH);
    }
```

The client code so far has set up the client window and the connection to the server, but we have not yet seen how anything happens. For this, we must look at the `actionPerformed` method, which is required since the `NameClient` class implements the `ActionListener` interface. When one of the buttons is clicked, the `actionPerformed` method is invoked because the `NameClient` class is registered as a listener:

```
// select an action depending on which button was pressed
        public void actionPerformed (ActionEvent ae)
        {
            Object buttonClicked = ae.getSource();
            try
            {
                if (buttonClicked.equals(goButton))
                {
                    processGo(); // respond to GO button
                }
                else if (buttonClicked.equals(quitButton))
                {
                    processQuit();  // respond to QUIT button
                }
            }
            catch (IOException e)
            {
                System.out.println("Problem with the server " + e);
            }
        }
```

Here, the `ActionEvent` argument `ae` allows us to find which object is the source of the event. In this case, the only relevant events are a click on one of the two buttons. If one of the two buttons is clicked, the corresponding method will be invoked to process this.

When the `Go` button is clicked, the method `processGo` is invoked. Its code is as follows:

```
// respond to Go button - User has requested an email address
private void processGo () throws IOException
{
    String usName;
    String emailAddress;

    // get the user name
    usName = userName.getText();

    // send it to the server
    toServer.println(usName);

    // receive reply
    emailAddress = fromServer.readLine();

    // display email address
    userEmailAddress.setText(emailAddress);
}
```

Here, the client sends the contents of the `userName` text field to the server. It then waits for the server to respond with the email address for that user and displays this in the other text field. To keep this example simple, we ignore the possibility that the `userName` text field may be blank. If this were the case, the server would simply reply with a message that the name had not been found.

Returning to the `actionPerformed` method, if the `Quit` button was clicked then the method `processQuit` would be invoked. The code is as follows:

```
// respond to Quit button
private void processQuit () throws IOException
{
    toServer.println(CLIENT_QUITTING);
    closeStreams(); // close streams to server
    socket.close(); // close socket connection to server
    System.exit(0); // close down client program
}
```

A special message is sent to the server to inform it that the client is terminating the connection. In response to this, we have seen earlier that the server will close the connection to the client. The client then closes the streams from its end using the helper method `closeStreams`. This is similar to the corresponding method in `NameServer`, with the code in the `NameClient` method as follows:

```
// close streams to and from the server
private void closeStreams () throws IOException
{
    toServer.close();
    os.close();
    fromServer.close();
    is.close();
}
```

The client code is run by a `main` method located in the separate class, `TestNameClient`, as follows:

```
public class TestNameClient
{
    public static void main (String[] args)
    {
        NameClient client1 = new NameClient("Name Service Client");
    }
}
```

In this case, we simply need to create a `NameClient` object in order to connect to the server and to set up the GUI. Because the client is driven by events (button clicks) from this point onward, there is no need to invoke any other methods and, in fact, the `NameClient` class does not offer any public methods. This is different from the example of a simple client in Section 7, where we invoked a `run` method to handle the interaction with the server because there was no GUI.

Before running the client, we need to start the name server. Otherwise, an exception will occur when the client tries to create a socket linked to the server. When the client and server above run successfully, the client will keep running until we click the `Quit` button, at which point it will close down. We can then start up another client, as the name server should still be running, and continue to interact with the server. In this example, there is no elegant way to close the server; we simply have to end the program by whatever means the environment offers to terminate programs.

Activity 9.8
Developing the full client–server name service.

SAQ 9

(a) What does it mean to specify the IP address "`127.0.0.1`" when creating a socket?

(b) Why is port number `3000` used in creating the socket in the client software in the example above?

ANSWERS ....

(a) The address "`127.0.0.1`" is an IP address with a special meaning. It does not correspond to any specific computer; it is known as the 'local host' or 'loopback' address. It indicates that the socket will communicate with a server located on the same computer as the client. This is often useful for testing on one machine before a system is deployed across a network.

(b) Port numbers `0` to `1023` are reserved for standard internet services. For example, HTTP requests use port `80`. When you write your own client–server software to operate across the internet, you should avoid reserved port numbers. Apart from this, port numbers can be chosen at random up to the maximum allowed value of `65534`, so port `3000` has no special meaning, in general.

9 Serving multiple clients

The server implementation in the previous section has a potentially serious problem: it deals with client connection requests one at a time.

In general, servers can have many clients requesting service at the same time. If a second client makes a connection request when a first client is being processed, then the second client will be queued and will be connected only when the first client has terminated its processing with the server. If the user of the first client is making infrequent service requests then it may be a long time before any other client is able to connect. At its most serious, there may be many clients queued and the server may reach its maximum queue size and disallow any more connections. In order to overcome this problem the code for the server should use *threads*.

Each connection that is accepted by the server should be handled by a separate thread. In this way, a number of threads could carry out the processing simultaneously. The first part of the code for a threaded class that handles a connection is shown below:

```java
public class ConnectionThread implements Runnable
{
    private Socket socket;
    private HashMap nameDatabase;

    // streams for connections
    private InputStream is;
    private OutputStream os;

    // writers and readers for communication
    private PrintWriter toClient;
    private BufferedReader fromClient;

    // protocol definitions
    static final String CLIENT_QUITTING = "Exit";
    static final String USER_NOT_FOUND   = "User not known";

    public ConnectionThread (Socket s, HashMap nameData)
    {
        socket = s;
        nameDatabase = nameData;
    }
```

```
public void run ()
{
    try
    {
        openStreams();

        processClientRequests();

        closeStreams();
        socket.close();
    }
    catch (Exception e)
    {
        System.out.println("Trouble with a connection " + e);
    }
}
```

The class `ConnectionThread` implements the `Runnable` interface; this means that it can operate as a thread, as discussed in *Unit 8*.

The most important part of the code is the `run` method, which contains similar code to that used in the `run` method of the server in the previous section. As before, this opens the input and output streams for the socket, processes the requests from this client and finally closes all the streams when the client has terminated.

The helper methods `openStreams`, `processClientRequests` and `closeStreams` are exactly the same as before, except that they are now private methods of the `ConnectionThread` class instead of being part of the `NameServer` class.

The main difference is that, since this is a threaded class, there may be a number of instances of this class running, each managing the connection to a different client and processing that client's requests.

Note also, the role of the constructor of the `ConnectionThread` class – it has two parameters that provide references to the socket to be used and the name database to which all threads must refer. These references are stored in instance variables by the constructor. We will see below where these references come from.

We also define a class called `ThreadedNameServer` to carry out initialization of the server and to control the creation of the `ConnectionThread` objects. The code for this class is as follows:

```
public class ThreadedNameServer
{
    private HashMap nameDatabase;
    private Thread connection;

    // use a high numbered non-dedicated port
    static final int PORT_NUMBER = 3000;

    // constructor
    public ThreadedNameServer ()
    {
        System.out.println("... Name Server starting up");
        nameDatabase = setUpNameDatabase();
    } // end constructor
```

```java
// set up name database and add sample data
private HashMap <String, String> setUpNameDatabase ()
{
    HashMap <String, String> db = new HashMap <String, String>();

    db.put("Gareth Williams", "G.R.Williams@java2.co.uk");
    db.put("Robert Thomas", "R.Thomas@java2.co.uk");
    db.put("William Wilson", "W.Wilson@java2.co.uk");
    db.put("Anne Land", "A.Land@java2.co.uk");
    db.put("Dave Phillips", "D.Phillips@java2.co.uk");
    db.put("Kirsten Davis", "K.L.Davis@java2.co.uk");

    return db;
}

// loop endlessly waiting for client connections
public void run ()
{
    // establish a ServerSocket
    try
    {
        ServerSocket ss = new ServerSocket(PORT_NUMBER);
        while (true)
        {
            // wait for a connection request
            Socket socket = ss.accept();
            connection = new Thread(new ConnectionThread
                                    (socket, nameDatabase));
            connection.start();
        }
    }
    catch (Exception e)
    {
        System.out.println("Trouble with a connection " + e);
    }
} // end method run
} // end class
```

The run method for the ThreadedServer class is similar in structure to the run method for the NameServer class in the previous section. The main difference is that client connections are not dealt with directly – a separate thread is created to handle the connection and communication with each client. We have thus separated the task of *listening for new clients* from the task of *actually dealing with each client*.

The main task of class ThreadedNameServer is now to do the listening, and to set up a thread for each client. Each thread is created using the ConnectionThread class, discussed earlier. The ConnectionThread constructor is passed two arguments: a reference to the socket that links to the client, and a reference to the name database. This ensures that the thread can communicate independently with this client, and can access the same name database as any other threads.

The `start` method of the thread object is invoked and it begins to execute independently. As for all threaded classes in Java, starting the thread executes the `run` method of the threaded object, in this case the `run` method of the `ConnectionThread` object, which handles all the communication with a particular client. The main server loop then returns to wait for another connection request.

Again, we also require a class containing a `main` method, which can be used to create and run the `ThreadedNameServer` object. A suitable class, called `TestThreadedNameServer`, is as follows:

```
public class TestThreadedNameServer
{
    public static void main (String[] args)
    {
        ThreadedNameServer server1 = new ThreadedNameServer();
        server1.run();
    } // end main
}
```

The `main` method creates a `ThreadedNameServer` object and invokes its `run` method. This causes the server to set up the name database and then to wait for suitable clients to connect. As each client connects, a new `ConnectionThread` object is created to handle that client. In this way, the server can handle many clients at once, in a responsive way. The number of clients is typically limited only by the resources of the system such as the amount of memory required, or the fact that response time increases with each new client, since the threads are sharing the system processor.

The case for threading has been presented using an extreme example: that of an unthreaded server with clients that take a long time to complete their requests. Even when the duration of a client connection is short there is a compelling requirement for threading to ensure a responsive service to multiple clients. This means that virtually all servers are threaded.

Activity 9.9
Using a threaded server.

SAQ 10

Threaded servers are clearly very useful for enhancing responsiveness when there are many clients.

(a) Can you think of any potential problems?

(b) Do these apply in the threaded server example above?

ANSWERS ....

(a) If the server threads servicing different clients have access to shared items of data, this data must be protected against potential corruption. This could happen if a thread updating this data was interrupted by another thread before its update was complete. This protection can be provided using the idea of synchronization, as explained in *Unit 8*.

(b) This problem does not arise in the example above. The only item of data shared between the threads is the name database and this cannot be modified by any of the clients.

10 Datagram communication

Earlier in this unit, you met the concept of a *connectionless transport* service when the User Datagram Protocol (UDP) was introduced. You will remember that such a mechanism can be error prone but is fast. Java contains a number of facilities for datagram transport. The class `DatagramPacket` defines objects that will contain the data to be sent using UDP. The class `DatagramSocket` implements connectionless message sending: it is a mechanism for launching datagram packets into the internet and for listening to incoming datagrams addressed to a particular port number.

In order to show how these facilities work we will look at a simple client and a simple server. The client just sends a number of messages to the server, which displays each message on `System.out`.

One of the complications of datagram transport is that all communication is via fixed-length byte buffers: what is sent by one entity is received exactly by another entity, including any padding at the end of the buffer.

In the example below, we send a string and have allocated a fixed-size buffer to hold the string. The data in the packet is simply the string, converted to byte format; the UDP packet header contains, amongst other things, the length of the data. The server can then extract enough information to enable it to retrieve the string from each packet it receives.

10.1 The client code

The code for the client is shown below:

```
import java.net.*;
import java.io.*;

public class DatagramClient
{
    // number of bytes in a UDP packet
    static final int UDP_PACKET_SIZE = 512;

    // port number of UDP service
    static final int PORT_NUMBER = 4000;
    private DatagramSocket datagramSocket;
```

```
// constructor
public DatagramClient ()
{
    try
    {
        // create a socket
        datagramSocket = new DatagramSocket();
    }
    catch (IOException e)
    {
        System.out.println("Trouble setting up
                            datagram socket" + e);

    }
}
// send a datagram containing a message
public void sendDatagramPacket (String message)
{
    DatagramPacket packet; // UDP packet

    // convert string to bytes
    byte[] toBeSent = new byte[UDP_PACKET_SIZE];
    toBeSent = message.getBytes();
    try
    {
        /* UDP packet contains the data, total length of data,
        destination IP address and destination port. */
        packet = new DatagramPacket(toBeSent, toBeSent.length,
                InetAddress.getLocalHost(), PORT_NUMBER);
        datagramSocket.send(packet);
    }
    catch (IOException e)
    {
        System.out.println("Trouble sending
                            datagram packet" + e);

    }
}
}
```

The DatagramClient has a simple constructor, which sets up a datagram socket to be used for sending datagrams. Because UDP does not set up a connection (unlike TCP) this socket does not require any details of the destination. Only the individual packets contain the destination details, as we shall see later.

The client class has one method, sendDatagramPacket, which has a string argument specifying the text of the message to be sent. The packet data is a string containing the message text. The first part of the method formats the data appropriately and stores the string in byte format in the buffer toBeSent. We then create a datagram packet containing this data together with the packet header information required by the UDP protocol. This header information includes the destination IP address and port number as well as the number of bytes of data. The packet is then sent via the datagram socket to the specified IP address and port number. In this example, we are assuming the server is on the local host, as we specify the destination address using the static method InetAddress.getLocalHost. This is an alternative to specifying the loopback address "127.0.0.1".

We test this class using the `main` method of class `TestDatagramClient`, which is as follows:

```
public class TestDatagramClient
{
    public static void main (String[] args)
    {
        // message to tell the server we are quitting
        final String CLIENT_QUITTING = "Client quitting";

        DatagramClient dc = new DatagramClient();

        // create and send some packets
        dc.sendDatagramPacket("Wish you were here");
        dc.sendDatagramPacket("Weather is lovely");

        // send a packet to tell the server we are quitting
        dc.sendDatagramPacket(CLIENT_QUITTING);
    }
}
```

This tests the class by creating a `DatagramClient` object and sending several messages, terminating with the message `CLIENT_QUITTING`. This is a special message to indicate to the server that the client has finished sending datagrams. Because UDP is connectionless, there is no need to close anything before the client program terminates – we just exit.

10.2 The server code

Of course, there is no point in running the client unless we have a server already waiting to receive its messages. So next we must look at how to program a server for UDP communication. All that the server does is to receive a datagram repeatedly, extract the text message and display it on `System.out`. The code for the server is as follows:

```
import java.net.*;
import java.io.*;

public class DatagramServer
{
    // number of bytes in a UDP packet
    static final int UDP_PACKET_SIZE = 512;

    // port number on which datagram is expected
    static final int PORT_NUMBER = 4000;

    // message which indicates that the client is quitting
    static final String CLIENT_QUITTING = "Client quitting";
    DatagramSocket datagramSocket;    // the datagram socket
```

```
public DatagramServer ()
{
    System.out.println("...Server starting");
    try
    {
        // set up datagram socket on port
        datagramSocket = new DatagramSocket(PORT_NUMBER);
    }
    catch (IOException e)
    {
        System.out.println("Problem setting up DatagramSocket:" + e);
    }
}

public void receiveData ()
{
    String message;            // message from client
    DatagramPacket packet;  // the packet of data received
    // buffer for receiving a fixed-size UDP packet,
    byte[] buffer = new byte[UDP_PACKET_SIZE];

    try
    {
        // continue reading packets until exit message
        boolean morePackets = true;
        while (morePackets)
        {
            // create an empty packet to receive the data
            packet = new DatagramPacket(buffer, buffer.length);

            // receive a packet from the client
            datagramSocket.receive(packet);

            message = new String(packet.getData(), 0,
                            packet.getLength());
            System.out.println("Message received is '" +
                            message + "'");
            morePackets = (!message.equals(CLIENT_QUITTING));
        }
        System.out.println("...Server Terminating");
    }
    catch (IOException e)
    {
        System.out.println("Problem receiving packet:" + e);
    }
}
}
```

The constructor for the `DatagramServer` class sets up a datagram socket on the same port number used by the client when sending the datagrams. Note the need to specify a port number in this case, unlike when setting up the datagram socket in the client code. This is because the server needs to know on which port to listen for incoming packets.

The main work of the server is carried out in the method `receiveData`. As long as it is expecting more packets, it creates an empty datagram packet and waits for a datagram to arrive on the specified port. It then stores that datagram in the empty packet and uses the `getData` and `getLength` methods of the `DatagramPacket` object to extract the message text from the datagram. It displays the message string on `System.out` before returning to wait for the next message. The server terminates when it receives the special message text from the client telling it that the client is terminating.

To run this class we use the `main` method of class `TestDatagramServer`, which is as follows:

```
public class TestDatagramServer
{
    public static void main (String[] args)
    {
        DatagramServer server = new DatagramServer();
        server.receiveData();
    }
}
```

This simply creates a `DatagramServer` object to set up the socket and invokes its `receiveData` method to enable it to accept datagram packets from the client. In this case, as we have seen, the server program terminates if the client sends its termination message. Alternatively, we could change the server code so that the server continues running in order to receive messages from other clients.

Activity 9.10
Communicating with datagrams: letter drops.

SAQ 11

What are the advantages and disadvantages of the UDP protocol for sending data across the internet?

ANSWER...

UDP (User Datagram Protocol) provides a raw packet-sending facility without any of the more sophisticated facilities of TCP. First, there is no initial 'handshake' to establish a connection between the two computers involved. If packets get lost or corrupted, they are not automatically sent again. So, in a faulty or busy network, some packets making up the communication may well not arrive or may contain incorrect data.

The potential advantage is that with fewer overheads for handshaking and data correction, UDP data should travel more quickly. If correctness is not essential and speed is important, such as in some digitized voice communications and other streaming media, then UDP may be appropriate.

Who uses UDP?

We all do! We have seen that UDP is more appropriate for sending limited amounts of data, where precisely correct receipt of that data is less important than speed of transfer.

UDP is used by the internet DNS, which we met earlier in this unit – this is the Domain Name Service, which looks up the IP address corresponding to a symbolic domain name. The amount of data exchanged in this process is typically small, normally consisting of one UDP packet in each direction, with a relatively low probability of an error occurring. Hence the handshaking overheads of setting up a TCP connection would be excessive and UDP is appropriate.

Some programs use both UDP and TCP. For example, the RealAudio service, from the RealNetworks company, allows the user to listen to an audio stream such as a radio programme. TCP is used to initiate a download connection to a RealAudio Player client. After the connection is established, the RealAudio server sends the audio data as a series of UDP packets. If a few data packets get corrupted or lost, this can be ignored with little effect on the overall quality of service to the user. This is preferable to pausing the audio stream while replacement packets are sent (as would happen with TCP) – such an interruption is likely to be perceived by users as a poorer service.

11 Summary

Before you can program internet applications, you need to know something about the internet. In this unit, we have seen how the internet is structured, described the concept of a client and a server and outlined how resources on the internet are accessed.

One of the features of Java is that its network API hides many of the technical details of the internet. We illustrated this with a demonstration of how easy it is to access URL-based resources from a Java program. We have considered how low-level internet programming is carried out in Java. The unit describes how sockets are implemented on both the client and the server, and how streams are used for communication of data between clients and servers. A name service was used as a programming example. Most servers are threaded to improve their performance and we have seen how a multi-client server can be developed in this way. The unit concluded by looking at how datagram communication is achieved in Java.

In general, in this unit we have looked at quite low-level programming approaches to distributed system development. These approaches are used when speed and efficiency are important. There are a number of other technologies in this area, such as distributed object technologies. However, they are outside the scope of this course.

LEARNING OUTCOMES

When you have completed this unit, you should be able to:

▶ write programs to access data from websites;

▶ outline how the internet is structured;

▶ explain the concept of a protocol;

▶ explain the roles of clients and servers;

▶ describe how resources on the internet are addressed;

▶ program clients and servers using sockets;

▶ implement a threaded server to handle multiple clients;

▶ program connectionless communication using datagrams.

Concepts

The following concepts have been introduced in this unit:

addressing, application protocol, client, connection-oriented service, connectionless service, datagram, distributed system, domain name, dotted quad notation, handshake, host, HyperText Transfer Protocol (HTTP), Internet Domain Name Service (DNS), Internet Protocol (IP), IP address, local host, loopback address, name service, numeric address, packet, packet header, packet switching, peer-to-peer (P2P), port, protocol, protocol levels, request, response, server, socket, symbolic address, system architecture, system protocol, TCP/IP, Transmission Control Protocol (TCP), Uniform Resource Locator(URL), User Datagram Protocol (UDP), web server.

Index

A

accept method 25, 29, 31

addressing 19
    dotted quad notation 19
    IP 19, 24
    numeric 19
    symbolic 19

application protocols 15

architectures 9
    client–server 10
    n-tier 10
    P2P 10

C

client queue 25

client–server 9–10, 24
    architecture 10
    exceptions 32, 37
    multi-threaded server 43
    multiple clients 33
    programming 26
    simple 28

connection-oriented service 17

connectionless service 17, 47

D

DatagramPacket 47

datagrams 18

DatagramSocket 47

distributed systems 9

DNS 20

Domain Name 20

dotted quad notation 19, 24

E

event-driven programming 38

exceptions 8, 32, 37
    MalformedURLException 8

F

File Transfer Protocol 15

flushing 30

FTP 15, 26

H

handshake 17

hosts 9

HTTP 10, 15

HyperText Transfer Protocol 10

HyperText Transmission
Protocol. *See* HTTP

I

internet 13

Internet Domain Name Service 20

Internet Protocol 14

IP 14–15
    addressing 19
    IPv4 19

L

listening 20, 25, 29, 45

local host 31, 48

loopback address 31, 48

M

MalformedURLException 8

N

name service 20

numeric addresses 19

P

P2P 10

packet switching 13

packets 14
    packet header, 14

peer-to-peer architecture.
See P2P

POP3 15

port 20

Post Office Protocol. *See* POP3

PrintWriter 29

protocols 13
    application protocols 15
    FTP 15, 26
    HTTP 15

IP 14–15
POP3 15
protocol levels 15
reliable 17
request 13
response 13
TCP 13–15, 17, 20
UDP 20, 48, 52

R

request 13

response 13

routing 14

S

ServerSocket 25, 29
    accept method 25, 29, 31
    client queue 25
    listening 25, 29

socket 21
    input and output streams 24

Socket class 24

streams 24

symbolic addresses 19

system architectures 9

T

TCP 14–15, 17, 20

TCP/IP 13

threaded servers 43, 46

Transmission Control
Protocol. *See* TCP

try–catch statement 37

U

UDP 20, 47, 52

UDP packet 18

uniform resource locator 6

URI 23

URL 6, 21, 23

User Datagram Protocol 17

W

web pages 6

web servers 10, 13